# This book belongs to

_____

This book is dedicated to my children - Mikey, Kobe, and Jojo.

Copyright © 2023 Grow Grit Press LLC. All rights reserved. No part of this book may be reproduced in any form without permission in writing from the publisher. Please send bulk order requests to info@ninjalifehacks.tv

Paperback ISBN: 978-1-63731-814-0
Hardcover ISBN: 978-1-63731-816-4
eBook ISBN: 978-1-63731-815-7
Board Book ISBN: 978-1-63731-817-1

Printed and bound in the USA.
NinjaLifeHacks.tv

by Mary Nhin

Ninjas are aware of surroundings,
And sensitive to sound.
To be a good ninja,
It's important to know what's around.

As a ninja, I'm always paying attention
To changes in the air.
The weather affects what we do,
And even what we wear!

On a **sunny** day, I see best,
My obstacles are nice and clear.
The air is fresh and easy to breathe,
I can easily conquer any fear.

I feel the sun's warmth,
On my back and the top of my head.
**Sunny** days make me feel energized,
I am able to run and spring ahead.

**Cloudy** days I can still run,
Even though the sky is less bright.
I look up in between the clouds
To gatch the glimpses of light.

The air feels a bit thicker,
When the clouds take over my view.
But even when it's gray out,
There is nothing I can't do!

**Rain** makes being a ninja harder,
When everything is slippery and wet.
I go to lunge as I normally would,
But then I slip because I forget.

BOOM!

But a ninja knows rain happens
When water drops form inside a cloud.
The pitter patter is almost peaceful,
Until I hear a **BOOM** that is loud.

A **thunderstorm** is coming in,
Lightning flashes through the sky.
As a ninja, I not only observe weather changes,
I could even tell you why!

**Thunder** cannot hurt a ninja,
Although it may seem frightening.
We take it as a sign,
To be cautious of the lightning.

As a ninja, I love when it's **snowing**,
It makes it easier to hide!
I play in it, make snowballs,
When it gets too cold, I go inside.

I love to practice in the snow,
To work on my chops and kicks,
But my favorite is not when it's **snowing**,
I love it most when the snow actually sticks!

Continue the learning with our fun lesson plans which include superpower skills practice, STEM activity, craft, and more! Visit ninjalifehacks.tv

 @marynhin  @officialninjalifehacks  #NinjaLifeHacks

 Ninja Life Hacks

 Mary Nhin   Ninja Life Hacks

 @officialninjalifehacks

www.ingramcontent.com/pod-product-compliance
Lightning Source LLC
Chambersburg PA
CBHW041525070526
44585CB00002B/93